RACE CAR LEGENDS

CHELSEA HOUSE PUBLISHERS

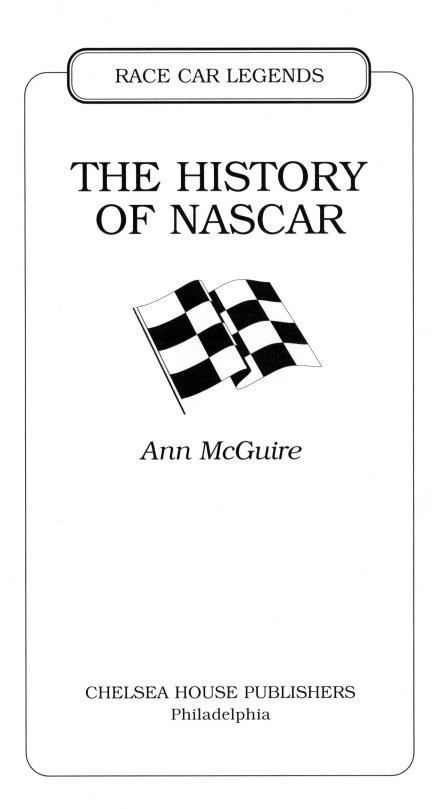

RACE CAR LEGENDS

THE HISTORY OF NASCAR

Ann McGuire

CHELSEA HOUSE PUBLISHERS
Philadelphia

Frontis: *Stock car drivers at the start of the 1998 Goody's 500 in Martinsville, Virginia. The race was one of 33 that marked NASCAR's 50th anniversary season.*

Produced by
21st Century Publishing and Communications, Inc.
New York, New York
http://www.21cpc.com

CHELSEA HOUSE PUBLISHERS

Editor in Chief: Stephen Reginald
Managing Editor: James D. Gallagher
Production Manager: Pamela Loos
Art Director: Sara Davis
Director of Photography: Judy L. Hasday
Senior Production Editor: LeeAnne Gelletly
Publishing Coordinator: James McAvoy
Assistant Editor: Anne Hill
Cover Illustration & Design: Keith Trego

Front Cover Photo: AP Photos/Grant Halverson
Back Cover Photo: AP Photos/Bob Jordan

The Chelsea House World Wide Website address is
http://www.chelseahouse.com

First Printing

1 3 5 7 9 8 6 4 2

Library of Congress Cataloging-in-Publication Data

McGuire, Ann.
    The history of NASCAR / by Ann McGuire.
    64 p.   cm.—(Race car legends)
    Includes bibliographical references (p. 63) and index.
    Summary: Surveys the history of the National Association for Stock Car
Automobile Racing.
    ISBN 0-7910-5414-4
    1. NASCAR (Association)—History Juvenile literature. 2. Stock car racing—
United States—History Juvenile literature. [1. NASCAR (Association)—History.
2. Stock car racing—History.] I. Title. II. Series.
GV1029.9.S74M34   1999
796.72'0973—dc21
[B]   99-31676
                                                                          CIP
                                                                           AC

CONTENTS

JEFF GORDON REWRITES THE RECORD BOOKS

Jeff Gordon clinched the 1998 Winston Cup championship before he even started the car for the NAPA 500, the 33rd and final race on the National Association for Stock Car Automobile Racing (NASCAR) premiere series. He'd done so by earning the most points for the season when he finished first a week earlier in the AC Delco 400 at the North Carolina Motor Speedway.

But Gordon, the poster boy of the new era of NASCAR, wasn't content with simply running the race and picking up his champion's trophy and check after the race. He and his crew had done that twice before and they were not happy.

Gordon won the 1995 and 1997 series championships, but despite those victories he and his teammates were extremely disappointed that they weren't able to end the 1997 season winning the race at Atlanta. This gnawed at Gordon and his crew chief, Ray Evernham. So this time they went to

Jeff Gordon leads the pack at the Bud at the Glen road race in Watkins Glen, New York, in August 1998. He went on to win the race and his third consecutive Winston Cup Championship, ensuring his place in the NASCAR record books.

Atlanta, knowing they had locked up their third championship and the millions of dollars that goes along with it, determined to also win the race. The trouble was, there were 40 other drivers who wanted to win just as badly.

Then it rained. And rained. And rained.

The race started after a rain delay and then was later stopped for more than two-and-a-half hours. The race was then started again only to have more rain fall.

"One thing I've learned about rain delays is do not go to sleep," Gordon commented later. "Do not go and take a nap because you come back and you're all groggy and can't keep your eyes open and you still wish you were in bed sleeping." So while other drivers retreated to their luxury motor homes to rest, Gordon played video games for hours.

"Rain delays can affect you," he added. "You get into a rhythm and you get going and all of a sudden you stop and you've got to come in and you don't know if you can get back into that rhythm or not."

After the second rain delay and four hours off the track, NASCAR officials summoned drivers back to their vehicles with the warning that only 25 more laps would be run. It was nearly midnight. About half of the track's original crowd remained in the stands, and even those folks were seriously soaked. Atlanta Motor Speedway officials had long ago turned on the lights, which had never been used for a stock car race in the history of the facility.

Before NASCAR officials restarted the race, all teams were required to make a pit stop. The track was dry, they said, but the pit area was way too wet for teams to make pit stops at full speed. Evernham, considered a genius as a crew chief, ordered his team to change all four of Jeff Gordon's tires. Other teams chose to change just two.

With 23 laps to go, Gordon weaved his way through the pack of cars ahead of him. Then Morgan Shepherd hit Gordon's car. Gordon wrestled to keep his car under control while Shepherd slammed into the wall. Following a five-lap caution period, the race was on again. Dale Jarrett zoomed past Gordon and into fourth place. "I thought that was the race," Gordon said afterward. "If Dale Jarrett gets by me I'm done."

Gordon wasn't done, however. He got right behind Jarrett's bumper and followed him to the front. As Gordon described the situation, "He worked his way up there pretty quick, and I worked my way up. . . . But even when I got up to him, I'd fade a little bit."

The two drivers, racing at speeds of more than 180 miles per hour, battled all the way around the 1.5-mile Atlanta Motor Speedway. Gordon, always plotting his next action, noticed Jarrett was having his own troubles. With six laps to go, Gordon made his move.

"All of a sudden, I saw his car start to slide up through the corners," Gordon said. "He couldn't keep it on the white line. I [could] put mine on the white line. Once I did, I got a great run off turn four. I was underneath him, and I knew this was the battle. This was the race right here."

Gordon passed Jarrett and led the final laps of the race. With Jarrett behind him, and the checkered flag his to take, Gordon radioed his team. "Way to go guys. We just tied Richard

Petty," he said. "What a year, what a year!"

Gordon pulled his car down the front stretch, stopped, and then mashed the gas while turning the wheel. The three-time champion spun wildly, filling the air with a cloud of tire smoke.

"They've been the team this year and they just beat us at the end right there," Jarrett said after the race. "You've got to give them credit because they do it right."

Jeff Gordon had just won his third Winston Cup title in just four years. Along the way he had earned his 13th win of the season, tying Richard Petty, the acknowledged king of stock car racing, for the most wins in a single season during the modern era. Gordon further secured his place in the sport's record books.

But Gordon's championship was much more than another statistic. It capped NASCAR's 50th anniversary season, a year in which the sanctioning body celebrated and promoted its formation five decades earlier. And in tying Petty's one-season win record and racking up a few others, including the most money ever won by a driver in a season, Gordon ensured himself his rightful place within the annals of NASCAR history.

Yet his championship is even more significant. With the refined driving skills and fearless nature that was also embedded in drivers before him, Gordon has taken the sport a step further. He's the first stock car driver ever to be included in national commercials alongside other popular sports figures. He's been featured in the famed "milk mustache" promotions, and has become a multi-million dollar promotional machine who appears on TV sitcoms and late night television shows.

Gordon, a handsome, well-spoken California native with a beautiful wife, is the face that leads NASCAR into its next 50 years. Looks notwithstanding, Gordon isn't much different from the daring men who preceded him on the track. He's had a life-long love affair with going fast and he's been willing to risk everything just to feel the thrill of victory. So too did the men who first started racing on back roads in the South more than 50 years ago.

Jeff Gordon celebrates his 1998 Winston Cup Championship after winning the NAPA 500 in Atlanta. During the 1998 series he won 13 races, tying Richard Petty's record for most races won in a single season.

RACING FROM
THE LAW

The foundation for Jeff Gordon's historic 13-win 1998 season and third Winston Cup title was actually laid 97 years earlier when the first races among early production models were held. In fact racing history may date back to the first two cars and two drivers who were willing to race.

Ford's racing history can be traced back to 1901, when founder Henry Ford defeated Alexander Winton in a race held in Grosse Pointe, Michigan. From there automobile racing took off, though often the vehicles were heavily modified for racing or created specifically for the sport.

While motorsports developed worldwide, stock car racing is a uniquely American creation. Its roots are firmly planted in the history of the country, more specifically the South. It was there that energetic men with spare time souped up their cars and raced each other in them.

These were not just regular guys, however. For the most part, they were lawbreakers.

Henry Ford with his first Ford automobile in 1896. In 1901 he defeated Alexander Winton in one of the first automobile races in history. Drivers have been modifying or building cars for racing ever since.

In the early part of this century, during a time called Prohibition, the selling or making of alcoholic beverages was banned by law. Despite these laws against making liquor, an entire hidden industry developed around the country to secretly keep making alcoholic drinks, then commonly called moonshine. Moonshiners, those who actually made the stuff, would concoct their mixtures using devices called stills, which were hidden well in the woods, mostly in the South.

The moonshiners would hire drivers to run the alcohol throughout the region. The drivers modified their cars to allow the liquor to be concealed and to carry as much of the valuable goods as possible. They also did whatever they could to add more horsepower to their cars in order to outrun the police when necessary.

Although Prohibition ended in 1933, the illegal manufacture of alcohol continued into the 1940s as moonshiners made and sold huge quantities of the intoxicating beverages to willing customers without paying the appropriate taxes to the government. Moonshine runners continued to take great pride in their ability to outrun any police officers who might catch up with them while on a delivery run.

Conversely the police would devise ways to catch the drivers, such as adding a clamp at the front of their patrol cars to grab onto the backs of the drivers' cars. Always one step ahead, moonshine runners were soon rigging their cars and attaching a small breakaway wire that would allow them to separate the car from the bumper whenever the police locked on.

Battles with police led to local legends of various drivers being faster than one another.

Eventually such discussions would lead to some sort of a bet that would then be settled in a makeshift race set up on vacant farmland or on a back-country road. Before the race started, the drivers would create an oval racetrack by driving around and around until they wore a path through the grass. The races were staged with no tickets or safety gear—nothing but a gathering of drivers who had been bickering for days about who had the fastest car.

Drivers were rough and the races rougher. They would bang and beat on each other until one driver was out in front. It wasn't unusual to have a race end and a fistfight begin. The races would draw locals who would creep up to the fenceposts and root for their favorite drivers. As with any event that draws spectators, shrewd businessmen took over and began staging the races and charging the fans admission. In turn the businessmen would pay the winning drivers a portion of the money received from ticket sales.

There were no formal rules, no inspectors to check out the cars, no safety equipment inside the cars, and no one to keep track of the promoters who held on to the ticket sales money. Occasionally, a dishonest promoter would run off with the cash before the race was over, leaving the drivers empty-handed and no doubt very upset. This combination of bad promoters and moonshine runners as drivers gave the sport of auto racing a decidedly bad name at its start.

At just about the same time that moonshine runners were engaging in their back-country races in the South, William Henry Getty "Big Bill" France, an auto mechanic from

Washington, D.C., had set his sights on Florida. While in Washington, France worked at a local garage as a mechanic and occasionally drove in some races. Like his brethren in the South, France had also been cheated by promoters who skipped out with his earnings or failed to pay him after a race. He often referred to one instance in 1930 when a promoter advertised a race with a purse of $500. After the race, in which France finished fourth, he was given $10. When he asked about the difference in the advertised purse and what was paid out to him and other drivers, the promoter told him the $500 figure was just to lure fans to the track.

In 1934, tired of the cold Washington winters and attracted by the growing interest in racing taking place in Florida, France packed up his wife Anne and their son Bill Jr., and they headed south. When they reached Florida they stopped in Daytona Beach, where France fell in love with the coast.

He was immediately drawn to the beach area, where several drivers had previously made land-speed runs on the hard sand. France quickly landed a job at a local service station and soon earned enough money to open his own garage in Daytona.

Still he couldn't shake the racing bug.

France was there in March 1935 when Sir Malcolm Campbell drove a supercharged V-8 rocket named Bluebird across the wide sands of Daytona Beach at speeds of up to 276 miles per hour. Later Campbell decided the beach wasn't long enough to continue his speed quest, so he relocated to the Bonneville Salt Flats in Utah where he continued his record-breaking land-speed runs.

This picture of former moonshine runner Junior Johnson was taken in 1964.

Moonshine Runner Turned Race Car Driver

Growing up in the Brushy Mountains of North Carolina, Junior Johnson ran his first race in the late 1940s. "A promoter organized a bunch of local boys who transported illegal moonshine to race their liquor-haulin' cars," Johnson recalled. "My family was in the liquor business and L. P. [Junior's brother] was a hauler. He wanted me to drive his car. L. P. figured one of two things . . . either I had more nerve than he did or I was crazier than he was."

There were about 20 cars at the race and Johnson finished second. The track where the race took place was dirt at the time. "As the race wore on it became rutted and soon was as rough as a plowed field." Johnson reminisced, "But I enjoyed myself. . . . I knew I wanted to do it again." Johnson's daredevil style of driving earned him the nickname "The Wilkes County Wildman."

Junior Johnson was destined to be a part of stock car racing for the next half century, becoming a legend in his own time. He ran his first NASCAR race in 1953. His line in the record book shows 341 starts, 50 victories, 71 other top-five finishes, and 47 poles earned by the time he retired from race car driving in 1966. Johnson went on to enjoy similar success as a team owner, claiming 140 victories and six Winston Cup championships before retiring from the sport entirely at the end of the '95 season.

The first 250-mile beach-road race for stock cars was held in Daytona Beach, Florida, in March 1936. Drivers who went too fast on the sand, like Bobby Sall (pictured in this amazing action shot), flipped over. Sall was knocked unconscious but was otherwise uninjured.

As a result, however, Daytona was no longer seen as the center of speed. Daytona Beach's community leaders felt the city needed a tourist attraction during the Great Depression era to boost the local economy, and car racing on the beach fit the bill. They soon began to make plans for a race on a course laid out partly on the beach and partly on a highway parallel to the beach. The first 250-mile beach-road race for stock cars was held in March

1936, with Bill France among the 27 drivers in the field.

The initial event was beset with problems. Drivers moving too slow got stuck in the sand, while those going too fast flipped over. Overall speeds for the race were, much slower than promoters anticipated, and to top it all off the tide came in before the race was scheduled to end. After 200 miles of the race were completed, one turn was completely blocked by stuck cars and waves, so the race was declared over. It took days before race officials made their final determinations and awarded the win to Milt "Red" Marion, who got $1,700 for the victory. France, who finished fifth, got $375, although he swore he passed Marion several times.

The following year, the community leaders turned the race over to the Elks Club, which really botched the event, giving the winner just $43. The local chamber of commerce decided that they needed someone to take over the event, so Bill France stepped in. He knew the race could make money if organized correctly, but he didn't have the financial resources to make the event a real success.

The following year, France staged the race and sold 4,500 tickets at 50 cents apiece. France's first attempt at race promotion was a modest but clear success and became the basis for today's NASCAR organization and the Winston Cup Series. France's first promotional efforts also laid the groundwork for Jeff Gordon's three championships.

BILL FRANCE'S DREAM

By the late 1940s, the concept of organized stock car racing began to take off all over the country, although the sport was for the most part located on the East Coast. However, for every sincere racing promoter, there was an unscrupulous one. The race car drivers put their lives, and often their family vehicles, on the line in each race. But they were still not guaranteed the promoter would be around at the end of the race to pay off the winner's purse. Bill France was very aware of how the bad promoters were hurting the sport.

At the same time, France's races on the beach at Daytona were booming. Judging from his own experiences and the reports he was receiving from tracks around the region, it appeared clear that there were eager audiences for car races. Early on, France got the idea of creating a national championship. At one point he even tried to promote the winner of the beach race as a national champion.

Bill France Jr. was awarded the Patrick Jacquemart Trophy in 1984 for his pioneering contributions to auto racing. France shared his father's passion for making NASCAR a well-organized, nationally respected sport.

However, he was told that without an overall sanctioning body with specific rules, the beach race winner could not have true national status.

So on December 12, 1947, with his vision of creating a nationwide ruling body for racing, and faced with the problem of crooked promoters, France gathered a number of his racing colleagues in Daytona Beach. He felt it was important for the group to join together to help the sport grow. Moreover, he believed it was essential for racing to have a clear set of rules that would keep the competitors and the cars on fairly equal terms. Likewise, he wanted to create a point system by which drivers could contend for a national championship.

The overriding focus of the meeting was that the parameters of the sport be set in order to make the competition fair. Before the meeting was over, France pitched one other radical idea. He wanted the drivers to race only the newest cars available, and not junkers. He wanted teams to use standard street cars, which could be purchased by the average person, and not specially built racing cars.

"Plain, ordinary working people have to be able to associate with the cars," France reportedly said. "Standard street stock cars are what we should be running."

Members of the group—34 promoters, drivers, officials, and other interested parties—voted to create a unified sanctioning body to oversee the growing sport of stock car racing. Red Vogt, a master mechanic, came up with a name for their organization: The National Association for Stock Car Automobile Racing (NASCAR). France was immediately elected president of the group.

On February 21, 1948, NASCAR was incorporated in Daytona Beach. NASCAR's first officially sanctioned race was held on the Daytona Beach road course and drew more than 10,000 spectators. "I think he was just trying to organize it," said Bob Latford, who as a kid sold programs for the Daytona Beach races. "It was so loose at the time."

The first race under NASCAR's new "strictly stock" rules was held on June 19, 1949, at a three-quarter–mile dirt track in Charlotte, North Carolina. This time there were 13,000 enthusiastic fans on hand to cheer on the drivers. Glenn Dunnaway of Gastonia, North Carolina, won the race, but he was then disqualified because the race car inspectors discovered that the 1947 Ford he was driving was illegally modified. The inspectors found a wedge jammed in the rear springs of Dunnaway's car, which back then was common in the cars used by moonshine runners. The wedges stiffened the springs, reduced the car's bounce, and increased its speed.

With the disqualification of Dunnaway's car, Jim Roper, from Kansas, who had finished second in a 1949 Lincoln, was awarded the victory and is in the record books as NASCAR's first-ever winner. He earned $2,000 for the win. As for Dunnaway, his fellow drivers felt he hadn't known about the spring wedge because the car was owned by someone else, and they donated a portion of their winnings to a fund for Dunnaway.

In NASCAR's first year of existence the cars that were eligible were Lincolns, Cadillacs, Oldsmobiles, and Hudsons. Those models were selected because they came equipped with massive, powerful engines. In keeping with the still-forming rules, they were driven essentially the same way they came off the showroom floor. Modifications were minimal—the cars raced complete with windshields, door handles, mirrors, bumpers, and even regular street tires—and safety features were non-existent. There were no rollbars, seat belts, cages, or any of the safety devices of today. In fact, many drivers actually drove their race cars to the track, used ordinary tape to create a number on the sides, and then raced. When it was all over, they'd pull the tape off and drive home.

There were eight races in all in the 1949 NASCAR season. The races were staged on a mix of dirt and paved ovals. In addition to Charlotte, races were also held at Daytona; Hillsboro, North Carolina; Langhorne, Pennsylvania; Hamburg, New York; Martinsville, Virginia; Heidelberg, Pennsylvania; and North Wilkesboro, North Carolina. NASCAR also sanctioned other races at dozens of tracks around the country.

NASCAR crowned Red Byron as its first series champion for winning two of the eight races, with Lee Petty taking second place. Among their competitors that year were Bob Flock, Curtis Turner, Jack White, and Gober Sosebee. Glenn Dunnaway finished the series in ninth position.

In the early days, stock car racing drew a variety of drivers from all walks of life. Many of the drivers were veterans of World War II, with some going from flying airplanes to piloting speeding race cars. "It was looser. Not as much money. There was more camaraderie amongst

the drivers, the crews, they were all in it together," recalled Bob Latford. "Nobody really had sponsors."

The inaugural "strictly stock" season gave birth to some of the racing families that endure in the sport today. From 1949 to 1960 Lee Petty finished consistently in the top 10 and won three of the championships. His son, Richard

Bill Rexford of Jamestown, New York, takes a practice run in 1951. He was the 1950 NASCAR series champion.

Three generations of the Petty family (seen here in 1979) have become NASCAR drivers. Lee Petty (left) began the tradition in the first NASCAR season; his grandson Kyle (with trophy) is now a Winston Cup driver. Kyle's father, Richard (right), won 200 races—a NASCAR record—and went on to become a team owner.

Petty, went on to earn 200 wins, the most for anyone in the history of the sport. Richard is now a team owner, his son Kyle is a Winston Cup driver, and Kyle's son Adam is also a driver on NASCAR's Busch Grand National series.

Likewise, Buck Baker made his NASCAR debut in 1949, driving in two races that year. His son Buddy later went on to become a Winston Cup standout and is now a television broadcaster for stock car races.

To say the first year was a successful one would be a gross understatement. The following year, NASCAR named the season's sanctioned events the Grand National Series and expanded it to 27 races, going as far north as Vernon, New York, and as far south as Daytona Beach. In many ways 1950 would be a clear indication of the way the series was to grow, but few, if any, could have predicted then how big the sport would later become.

NASCAR GAINS
A FOLLOWING

T he 1950s opened with a flourish for the sport of stock car racing. NASCAR's schedule in the first year of the decade more than doubled from the inaugural year. More importantly, the sport was starting to attract a following. Fans, who had started watching racing at makeshift tracks in open farmland, moved with the drivers to the better-organized racing facilities. Still, in the beginning many of the tracks were simply dirt outlets, primarily used for other purposes and converted into racing venues.

In 1948, in what could be pegged as one of the clear signals that folks other than Bill France saw a future in the sport, Harold Brasington decided to build a racetrack in Darlington, South Carolina. It took two years to build the 1.25-mile egg-shaped track on an open piece of land. The track was built with its distinctive shape because at the time Brasington was constructing it he had to preserve an existing minnow pond. In 1950 the spectacular Darlington Raceway opened as the first-ever paved

Darlington Raceway in South Carolina opened in 1950 and was the first paved track constructed for the NASCAR Grand National Series. The track is still famous among Winston Cup drivers, who call it "Too Tough to Tame," as it causes problems for even the most experienced drivers.

track built specially for NASCAR's then-fledgling Grand National Series.

Seventy-five cars participated in the first event. It took 15 days to qualify all of them. Some 25,000 fans, who bought tickets in advance, showed up for the race.

Johnny Mantz, driving a car he co-owned with Bill France, won the inaugural Southern 500 and earned $10,510 for the win. Today Darlington still stands as one of the showplaces of NASCAR's Winston Cup Series. The track is dubbed "Too Tough to Tame" for its difficulty and ability to turn even the best driver's day into a nightmare.

The success of the first-ever Southern 500 at Darlington sent shock waves throughout the business. The construction of that track created a ripple effect, launching the development of other facilities around the region.

Despite the increase in interest, NASCAR as a sanctioning body was still an unfamiliar entity. Folks knew about specific races, such as the Southern 500 or the Daytona Beach races, but NASCAR as a whole was for the most part unknown.

The concept of making a living racing cars was also still far off for many drivers. The best drivers—those who could consistently win races and preserve their equipment—were able to make a modest living, but for most racing was only a step above being a hobby. When the races were over, most drivers returned to their day jobs. Many, of course, were mechanics who raced on weekends or whenever they could. They were in the sport because they loved the competition and, perhaps more importantly, they craved going fast.

Indeed, none of today's common characteristics of racing existed in the early 1950s. There were no huge tractor-trailers to haul cars and equipment from race to race. Drivers didn't depend on pilots to fly them to the events in their personal planes. Teams were not able to spend millions on fancy paint schemes, color-coordinated uniforms, or decorative souvenirs. The drivers themselves were a rag-tag bunch at best. Off the tracks they were mechanics, truck drivers, welders, and the like.

With each successive year, NASCAR continued to expand its schedule. By 1955 NASCAR sanctioned 45 events at 32 different racetracks. To compete, drivers would travel around for weeks at a time. It wasn't unusual for them to race two or three nights in a single week, often going as far north as Canada and as far south as Daytona Beach. And after each race, they'd pack up and head to the next event.

"We'd be gone two weeks," said former driver Cotton Owens, who won nine races in a career that started in 1950 and ended in 1964. "We had to find the cheapest [motels]. You didn't have the bigger pit crews they've got today. It was a strain at the time."

The drivers had to bring not only their cars to the races but also virtually everything else they would need along the way, including gas. They also had to repair any damage that their vehicles might have sustained in the races while on the road. If they stayed in a hotel, it was not at all unusual to find crews repairing cars in the parking lot.

"We had to haul all our own fuel we [were] going to burn," Owens later recalled. "We had to truck all of our stuff. We used a tow-bar [a device to tow a car]. None of us had a one-ton truck, we had to borrow one."

There also wasn't a lot of money in the sport at that time. The amount the usual race paid to win—anywhere from a few hundred to a few thousand dollars—is much less than a driver would get today for finishing in last place in any of the Winston Cup events. Drivers had to race frequently to make money and to gain points to win the championship. "We were all just skimping to get by," Owens said.

Despite the shortage of money, the series was never short on fun. On the road and at the tracks, the drivers and crew members were generally more willing to help each other out. "It was good times," Owens recalled. "Everybody enjoyed themselves. It was like one big family."

On the track, drivers such as Curtis Turner, Speedy Thompson, and Herb Thomas were becoming high-flying daredevils, usually without safety equipment. And, because the cars did not have power steering, drivers tended to be bigger, heavier, and physically stronger.

During 1955 the sport got its first taste of sponsorship and major team funding. Carl Kiekhaefer, a Mercury boat motor manufacturer, provided his drivers with financial backing, top-notch equipment, and testing facilities, thus creating the concept of sponsorship. Kiekhaefer had gotten into racing to learn more about motors, which he thought could translate back to his Mercury outboard motors for boats. His cars carried the phrase "Mercury Outboards" on the side. However, Kiekhaefer eventually realized he was helping sell more Mercury cars than his outboard motors, so he changed the lettering to read "Kiekhaefer Outboards."

Later Kiekhaefer would become the first multi-car team owner when he raced upwards of five cars in some competitions. Today multi-car teams are the norm, although it took 40 years for Kiekhaefer's concept to really take off.

Not all teams were as lucky and as well funded as Kiekhaefer's. Many barely got by and only survived from race to race. "We owned our own cars," said Marvin Panch, who won 17 races during a career that spanned 15 years. "We didn't have fat sponsors to take care of us. Once and a while, one of the local dealers would give us $100 or $200. It sure helped."

Tracks of all sizes staged races around the country. Darlington, with its paved 1.25 miles in South Carolina represented the top end of the scale, while the half-mile dirt oval at the Monroe County Fairgrounds in Rochester, New York, represented the bottom. Many races were still held on dirt tracks as part of country fairs.

However, the track construction boom was well underway. NASCAR president Bill France wanted a showplace of his own. He also wanted to get his premiere race off the beach and onto a legitimate venue. So in 1953 he created Daytona International Speedway Corporation to develop a 2.5-mile, high-banked paved oval away from the sea in Daytona. France got a 99-year lease on the property and sold 300,000 shares of stock for $1 apiece. He also borrowed $600,000 from an oil millionaire.

Ground clearing for the project started in 1957. The track was built at a cost of $3 million, which is very little compared to today's racing facilities that cost upwards of $200 million to build. The final beach-road race was held in 1958. The following year France opened the Daytona International Speedway, a completely paved facility, and the inaugural Daytona 500 was run on February 22, 1959.

The drivers were enamored of the new track. Since it was longer, wider, and all paved it allowed the drivers to go more than 30 miles per hour faster than they had ever driven on a race track before, and three cars could drive around the turns side-by-side.

In true NASCAR fashion, the first Daytona 500 ended in a photo finish between Lee Petty and Johnny Beauchamp. It took NASCAR officials three days to ultimately decide that Petty was the winner.

The opening of Daytona, combined with the unveiling of a handful of other tracks in successive years, helped lay the groundwork for the sport today. However, even by 1960, it was still far from a full-time job for most drivers, though NASCAR as an institution was showing signs that it would be around to stay.

Slowly the sport was gaining national attention and drivers were racing their hearts out. Though NASCAR was sanctioning 52 events, drivers would enter other unofficial races. Unlike today, where teams on the top levels of the series are limited in where they can race, drivers back then would race any time and anywhere. Of course they wanted to accumulate points for the championship, but they also needed to make money. In the '50s, '60s, and even into the '70s, it wasn't unusual for local tracks around the country to stage midweek events, which would welcome appearances by the big guns of NASCAR.

New drivers came along with names like Ned Jarrett, Fred Lorenzen, and Junior Johnson.

In 1961, television, a key factor in the success of NASCAR today, first covered racing when ABC aired a portion of the Firecracker 400 from Daytona as part of its popular *Wide World of Sports* series. Although it would be more than a decade before viewers would get to see an entire race covered live on television, the ABC coverage did get the ball rolling.

On the track, both car makers and drivers started to become a little more safety conscious. Rudimentary roll bars, often made from plumber's pipe, started to appear in cars. Drivers also started using makeshift seat belts. Some even fitted their cars with airplane

Johnny Beauchamp (73) and Lee Petty (42) were neck and neck at the first Daytona 500 race in 1959. Drivers liked the Daytona International Speedway because the track let them go faster than ever. The average speed for this first race was 135.75 miles per hour.

In 1961 ABC was the first network to air coverage of NASCAR racing. Other networks eventually followed, but more than 10 years would pass before an entire race was televised live.

harnesses to keep them from flying around the car during a crash.

Still, accidents and even deaths sometimes occurred. In 1964 Glenn "Fireball" Roberts, one of the sport's best drivers and prominent personalities, was involved in a multi-car wreck at Charlotte. His car's metal fuel tank ruptured, and soon Roberts's car was engulfed in flames. Ned Jarrett, Roberts's best friend, was also involved in the crash. Jarrett freed himself from his own car and rushed to his friend's, which by then was an inferno. Roberts eventually got out of the car but later died due to his injuries.

Roberts's death, like those of other racing drivers, made NASCAR officials and suppliers of racing parts and equipment think more about safety. By 1965 the tiremaker, Firestone, unveiled a new rubber fuel-cell bladder that drastically reduced the threat of fire. The device replaced the traditional steel fuel tanks. A form of the bladder is still in use today and is widely credited with saving the lives of many drivers.

Meanwhile automakers also learned from the sport. They quickly realized that a race driver doing well in a specific brand of car could help push showroom sales. Somewhere along the line the term "Win on Sunday, Sell on Monday" popped up as carmakers saw a benefit in racing. Soon car manufacturers were sponsoring their own teams and funding operations so drivers and teams would use their cars. Car makers provided significant help to such teams as Petty Enterprises, Bud Moore Engineering, and Holman-Moody.

Corporate sponsorship was also making greater inroads into the sport. Most teams were

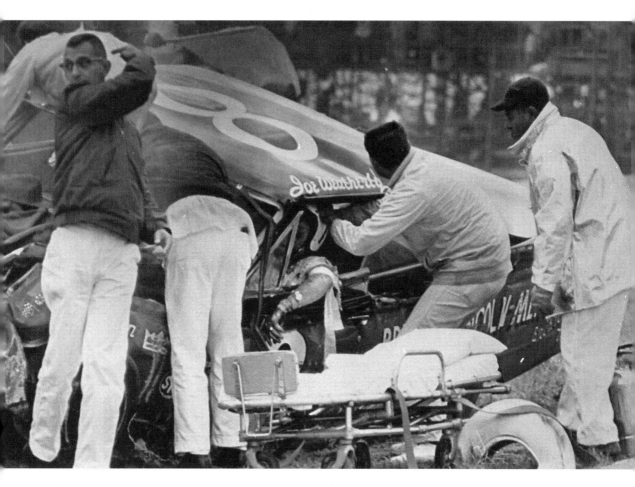

In 1964 racing accidents claimed the lives of several drivers, including Glenn "Fireball" Roberts and Joe Weatherly (pictured here as workers try to free him from the wreck). This led to a new emphasis on safety among NASCAR officials and equipment manufacturers.

getting some limited form of financial support from local car dealers, insurance companies, and small firms that wanted to capitalize on the rising popularity of stock car racing and the visibility it could afford their businesses.

Still, NASCAR held on to some of its roots. Small dirt tracks located at fairgrounds around the country remained part of the series, even as races expanded into facilities like Daytona, the Charlotte Motor Speedway, and the Atlanta Motor Speedway.

Nine years later, after having successfully opened the Daytona International Speedway in 1959, Bill France was about to upstage himself. He started construction on a much bigger and faster facility just east of Birmingham, Alabama. On May 23, 1968, construction of the superspeedway began on a 2,000-acre site in Talladega, Alabama. The new 2.66-mile, high-banked facility opened on September 13, 1969, to a swarm of controversy. Many of the drivers boycotted the first race claiming they were in danger because of the higher speeds and the threat of tires blowing out during the event. Bill France, angered at the boycott, got into one of the race cars and zoomed around the track himself.

The first event at Talladega was held, however, without the participation of some of stock car racing's regular drivers. Richard Brickhouse went on to win the inaugural race, collecting $24,550 for his efforts.

NASCAR staged its last race on dirt in 1970 in Raleigh, North Carolina, shedding one piece of its roots in an effort to progress toward the future. Over a period of 22 years, NASCAR had gone from a rag-tag bunch of racers to a serious sports organization. What was ahead, however, would shake NASCAR's foundation and set the stage for an unprecedented period of growth for the sport as a whole.

New Leaders
and Drivers Emerge

NASCAR's fortunes and future changed dramatically, and mostly for the better, in the years 1971 and 1972. During that short time span, Bill France turned the organization over to his son, NASCAR got a major sponsor, and the series was pared back to a modest 31 events.

By 1971 Bill France was tiring of running the sport he created. He was ready to step aside and let someone else take over. That someone, of course, was his son, Bill France Jr. The younger France had spent significant portions of his life around the raceway. As a teenager, he swept offices, sold programs, and cleaned restrooms. Later, after a stint in the Navy, he returned to the family business where he would remain. He had never intended to go into the business, but he had never really had any plans to do anything else, either.

On January 10, 1972, Bill France Jr. took over NASCAR from his father at what would ultimately prove to be a pivotal time in the sport's history. The

Bill France Jr. (left) helped change the face of NASCAR when he took over its leadership from his father in 1972. France is still active in racing as the head of the International Speedway Corporation. Here he talks to Rob Dyson (right), one of the new generation of race car drivers and owners.

transition wasn't without problems. Certain drivers and team owners liked the elder France better. They trusted him and knew little about Bill Jr. But over time the new president won their confidence.

One of Bill Jr.'s first major challenges was to make sure the NASCAR organization would continue in the wake of the automakers' recent decision to pull out of the sport. Carmakers Ford, General Motors, and Chrysler had heavily funded teams in the past, paying the costly bills for engines, drivers, crews, and testing. They therefore wanted more control of the sport, but the France family was determined not to give it to them.

With the carmakers out, France needed to find a new source of funding, and fast.

A year earlier, Junior Johnson, then one of the sport's best drivers and a national figure, had convinced tobacco giant R. J. Reynolds to sponsor a couple of races in the series. R. J. Reynolds started out wanting to sponsor Johnson's team, but Johnson wisely steered him toward NASCAR. Johnson's overture to R. J. Reynolds came at a time when tobacco companies were being banned from advertising on radio or television.

Johnson and NASCAR eventually convinced R. J. Reynolds to sponsor the entire series. The company, seeking a way around the government restrictions on advertising, agreed. The company was to put up $100,000 annually for a driver's points fund and to promote racing around the country. Almost overnight, tracks were repainting their facilities in the red and white of R. J. Reynolds's Winston brand, giving birth to the Winston Cup Series.

R. J. Reynolds (seen here in a 1910 photograph) founded the R. J. Reynolds Tobacco Co., the maker of Winston cigarettes. In 1971 the company was the first to sponsor an entire NASCAR series, which was named the Winston Cup. Soon, other non-automotive sponsors followed suit. The funds and the marketing clout that these large corporations brought to the sport greatly helped increase NASCAR's visibility nationwide.

In addition, a corporation with the reach of R. J. Reynolds helped give NASCAR the marketing clout it previously lacked. Moreover, seeing R. J. Reynolds in the picture convinced other national, non-automotive sponsors to put their money into racing.

When NASCAR cut its schedule from 48 events in 1970 to 31 in 1972, it produced what is now referred to in stock car racing as the "modern era." By eliminating 17 races, teams were given more time to prepare for each event which led to better competitions on the tracks. Gone were the days when teams had to run two

Darrell Waltrip holds a fake newspaper that declares him the 1982 Winston Cup champion. Waltrip always bragged about his ability to win races. And his driving skills and understanding of race cars proved him right time after time.

or three races a week to compete for the title.

New tracks were being added to the circuit. In 1974 NASCAR held its first race at the Pocono International Raceway in Long Pond, Pennsylvania. The track, which had opened in 1969 as a .75-mile oval, was expanded to its current 2.5-mile triangular configuration in 1971, and held its first big-time NASCAR race in 1974.

Throughout the '70s and early '80s, a second

generation of race car drivers started to emerge as NASCAR's newest stars. In 1972, Darrell Waltrip entered the Winston Cup ranks and almost immediately won new fans while angering other drivers. Waltrip was an upstart driver out of Tennessee. He was willing to say exactly what he was thinking to just about anyone who would listen, and he was also able to back up his boasts with wins on the track.

"Darrell is very, very close to being almost a genius as far as understanding the race car; He's a tremendous mechanic," said Buddy Baker, who had driven against Waltrip. "The first time I ever heard him speak, he walked up to a radio show, grabbed the microphone and said, 'I'm Darrell Waltrip, I'm here to replace Richard Petty.' I think Darrell really believed that."

The '70s seemed to be owned by a handful of drivers; among them were David Pearson, Richard Petty, Benny Parsons, Cale Yarborough, and Bobby Allison. They were tough-as-nails competitors who still remain high on NASCAR's list of drivers with the most wins. For example, Yarborough won 28 races in two years and had two consecutive championship seasons.

At the time, the cars themselves were going through a transition as well, from stock cars to vehicles built just for racing. During the '70s the cars still maintained some of their street-legal characteristics, although underneath the sheet-metal they were pure race cars. The transition would continue into the early '80s.

In 1978 NASCAR took another major step forward when stars of the sport were invited to the White House to visit with President Jimmy Carter and First Lady Rosalyn Carter. The visit was significant because it made clear that stock car racing was a legitimate sport and should be considered alongside the traditional ones like football, basketball, and baseball.

In addition to the substantial involvement of R. J. Reynolds, NASCAR may have gotten its next biggest push forward with the help of long-time broadcaster and race fan Ken Squier. For years, Squier had been anchoring radio telecasts of racing events, but he longed for television coverage. Squier was able to convince the folks at CBS to air the 1979 Daytona 500 from start to finish. No other broadcaster had ever carried a complete Winston Cup race, and many network executives wondered if viewers would stick with a telecast that could last five hours or more.

CBS, as well as NASCAR, also got a lucky break when a massive blizzard hit the Northeast, keeping viewers locked in their homes for most of the weekend. Many of them watched the Daytona 500.

And what a race they got. Donnie Allison and Cale Yarborough went into the final lap battling for the lead, well in front of the rest of the cars. Allison had the advantage down the backstretch but had Yarborough on his tail setting up to pass. They ran door-to-door around the track and then touched, sending both cars slamming into the wall.

Petty took the lead, won the race, and earned his sixth Daytona title. But behind him, amidst the wrecked cars, Yarborough and Donnie and Bobby Allison were fighting. Flailing wildly, they angrily punched and kicked at each other. Meanwhile, shocked viewers watched the dramatic episode from their homes.

The Daytona 500 fight, now legendary, was

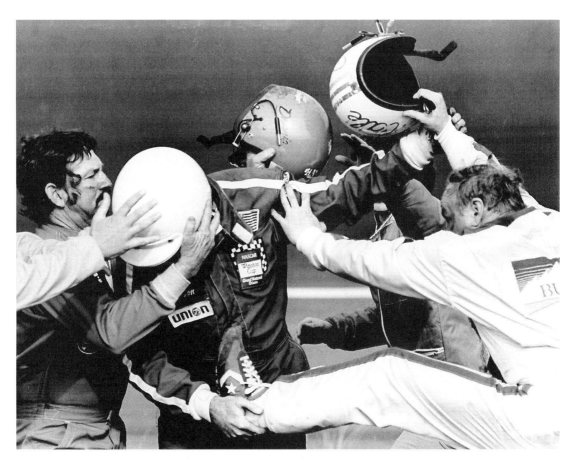

just one highlight of the first stock car race televised from start to finish. The race served as a wake-up call for television executives, who until then believed racing wasn't viable programming for TV. Up to that point, it seemed only folks in the Southeast really and truly appreciated the sport. After the CBS telecast, viewers beyond the South began to gain an entirely new appreciation for stock car racing. Although a bit tentatively at first, major media outlets around the country began following the racing events. At the time, any coverage was a leap above the levels that existed in 1970.

The famous 1979 fight between Cale Yarborough (right) and Bobby Allison (center). Yarborough collided with Donnie Allison (left) on the last lap of the Daytona 500, taking both drivers out of the race. Television viewers watched the fight from their living rooms as part of the first stock car race televised from beginning to end.

Then in 1981 a start-up channel called the Entertainment and Sports Network was launched. The new network, later to become ESPN, was flush with airtime it needed to fill and hungry for opportunities. At the same time, track owners looking to boost their income were more than willing to sell the broadcasting rights to the races at their facilities. At the time, broadcast rights went for as little as $50,000 a race. Today, some races cost broadcasters upwards of $10 million for the rights.

In 1983 CBS incorporated the use of an in-car camera during its coverage of the Daytona 500. Carl Yarborough carried the first in-car device, which at the time was bulky and unable to offer several views. However, the pictures fans got to see at home were dramatic.

"The city people looked at motorsports and said big deal, we all drive cars," Squier said. "The cars looked slow on TV. But then you rode around with Cale Yarborough and realized he looked like a helmsman steering his ship at 200 miles per hour." Five years later, CBS introduced tiny in-car cameras, dubbed "lipstick" cameras because their size and shape was similar to lipstick cases. These little cameras laid the groundwork for the multiple cameras and camera angles available during today's racing telecasts.

Meanwhile the new generation of NASCAR stars was making their mark. In 1980 Dale Earnhardt, the son of former racer Ralph Earnhardt, earned his first Winston Cup championship. In the next two years, Darrell Waltrip stepped in to win back-to-back titles. In 1984, Terry Labonte won the championship. Before the decade was over, Earnhardt would win two

more championships, Waltrip another, and Bill Elliott and Rusty Wallace would each win one.

The new generation of drivers was strong, but some of the elder statesmen would not be outdone. In 1984, before a crowd that included President Ronald Reagan, Richard Petty, the king of stock car racing, won the Firecracker 400 at Daytona to earn his record 200th win, a feat that has yet to be surpassed 15 years later. In 1983 Bobby Allison won the championship, demonstrating that the previous group of standout drivers still had much to contribute to the sport. By the dawn of the 1990s NASCAR proved it was still going strong.

Richard Petty has a lot to celebrate after winning his 200th NASCAR race at the Firecracker 400 at Daytona in 1984. To date, his record-breaking achievement has never been surpassed.

THE BOOM YEARS

While the popularity and growth of NASCAR has continued steadily throughout its history, no other decade comes close to reaching the level of attention the sport of stock car racing has received during the '90s.

Thanks to a combination of factors—sponsors, television, and NASCAR's efforts to grow—stock car racing clearly moved from being a regional form of entertainment to a full-fledged national sport vying for space on newspaper pages with football, basketball, baseball, and hockey.

For the first 40 years NASCAR was something of an afterthought for sports editors. But in the '90s, racing became real in the minds of many who had paid it no attention in the past. Following the lead of ESPN, other new cable channels, such as The Nashville Network (TNN) and TBS, began buying up the rights to races. Eventually, every NASCAR Winston Cup race was broadcast live. This shift to the live airing of every race helped to dramatically

The popularity of NASCAR events skyrocketed during the 1990s. No longer a regional sport, racing now has media coverage and devoted fans of all ages nationwide.

NASCAR has moved from rural tracks to urban areas. Here real estate developer Donald Trump (left) and Bill France Jr. hold a press conference to announce the development of a 75,000-seat track in the New York metropolitan area.

boost the sport's image, not only with racing fans and television executives but also with the sponsors that made racing possible.

The sport has moved into several major metropolitan regions throughout the '90s, including Los Angeles, Dallas, and the Northeast. There is even discussion about a new track—Trump Superspeedway—being built right in the New York City area—the largest TV market in the country.

Team sponsorship went from being a nice bonus for a team owner in the mid-80s to a necessity in the '90s. With the cost of racing spiraling upward, teams needed corporate backers more than ever. At the start of the decade, a company could back a competitive team for $2 million. By the end of the decade, top teams would command upwards of $10 million from a major sponsor. It didn't take major corporations long to figure out that with all of the races being aired on national television, team sponsorship was a good investment. In backing a team the companies not only got exposure to NASCAR's extremely loyal fans at the track but also the equivalent of free television time when their drivers ran up front.

The sport immediately began to lure major non-automotive consumer product companies such as Tide, Wrangler, Hardee's, and Folger's. Later, as sponsors got savvier about their investments in race teams, they also began heavily promoting their involvement with the sport off the track. Now it's common to walk down an aisle at a typical supermarket and find many products with a reference to NASCAR on the packaging. The additional off-track marketing also helps build exposure for the sport.

During the '90s NASCAR also benefited from troubles that hit other sports. Baseball, for example, got a black eye from a players' strike and some unfortunate instances of players' unsportsman-like activities. Hockey and football also had their own union troubles. So far stock car racing has avoided the union issues that have faced other sports. Generally speaking, the drivers and owners have been able to avoid controversy and resolve their issues, which has helped build a good image for stock

During the late 1990s sales of licensed NASCAR merchandise have increased from hundreds of thousands of dollars to close to a billion dollars a year. Popular stores, such as the one pictured here, carry a huge variety of items with a racing theme.

car racing in the minds of the fans, the corporate sponsors, and the media.

NASCAR also became a licensing phenomenon in the mid- to late '90s. Sales of toy racing cars, T-shirts, jackets, hats, key chains, and more with drivers' names, colors, and likenesses are reaching the $1 billion mark, putting the sport in line with the National Hockey League in terms of overall sales. That's a far cry from 1990, when sales of licensed merchandise were measured in terms of hundreds of thousands of dollars, not millions and billions.

The interest shown by corporate America, television, and the fans resulted in unprecedented growth at the tracks. During 1991, 3.38 million fans attended NASCAR's 33 events in the Winston Cup series. In 1998 the number of spectators reached nearly 7 million.

In terms of competition, the early '90s are notable for a couple of reasons that grew out of the 1992 season. In that year, driver Alan Kulwicki, who owned his own team, won the series championship in the final race of the season at Atlanta. Kulwicki's feat was significant because he had earned the title on his own by sticking to his own goals despite several seasons of struggling. He had turned down chances to drive for better-funded teams to remain his own boss. That season, his determination paid off.

Kulwicki's championship season was overshadowed less than a year later by his death. Kulwicki was killed in an airplane crash while heading to a race at the Bristol Motor Speedway. A few months later, the sport would be rocked again by the death of Davey Allison, a second-generation driver, who was killed while flying his own helicopter from a practice session at the Talladega Superspeedway near his hometown in Alabama.

The 1992 season also marked the finale for Richard Petty, who after 200 wins decided to retire. Jeff Gordon, an upstart driver from California by way of Indiana, also debuted in the Winston Cup series that year.

During that same year, NASCAR pushed its influence northward by staging its first-ever race at the newly renovated New Hampshire International Speedway, a 1.058-mile oval in

Louden, New Hampshire. The track was originally built in 1990 on the site of the Bryar Motorsports Park, which had opened in the 1960s. NASCAR sanctioned its first Winston Cup race there on July 11, 1993, and it was a tremendous success. Rusty Wallace won the event before a packed house. Despite talk of NASCAR's being a Southern sport, folks in New Hampshire turned out in droves to get tickets to the debut event and the events that followed. People lined up for hours for the Winston Cup races, guaranteeing sell-outs for every event.

Dale Earnhardt earned his seventh Winston Cup title in 1994 to tie Richard Petty's streak. Also in 1994, NASCAR held its first race at the Indianapolis Motor Speedway, the long-time home of open-wheel Indy style race cars. The race was significant because it took NASCAR to what was clearly hallowed ground to motorsports enthusiasts.

Then in 1995, Gordon, a handsome, well-spoken driver, earned his first Winston Cup title. In only his third full season on the circuit and then just 24 years old, Gordon proved he would be a driver to contend with for many years to come. Paired with New Jersey native Ray Evernham as his crew chief, on some days Gordon made winning a Winston Cup race look easy. Despite the many victories, off the track Gordon and Evernham maintained a race-by-race outlook.

Going into the final race of the season at Atlanta, Gordon had a 147-point lead over Earnhardt. In a way it was the kid taking on the champion—NASCAR's latest good guy going after a living legend, a driver best known on the tracks as "the Intimidator."

Gordon finished the last race in 32nd place, although he had already amassed enough points to assure himself the title. At 24 he earned $4.3 million on his way to becoming the youngest champion in the modern era.

Gordon wasn't the only driver to surface during the 1990s. Also emerging and making names for themselves were folks like Jeff and Ward Burton, Bobby Labonte, Jeremy Mayfield, Michael Waltrip, Dale Jarrett, Ernie Irvan, and Ted Musgrave.

Among the newcomers, Gordon stood out. With help from a team of managers and advisors, Gordon was able to transcend motorsports and be counted among the top sports stars of his day. Gordon's good looks and fierce competitiveness helped attract companies like Pepsi, which put him in commercials alongside such household names as Shaquille O'Neal and Deion Sanders. No other driver in the history of racing had been paired with superstars of other sporting events like this.

Gordon became the first driver to become a truly national spokesman for the sport, with his image appearing on billboards, in newspapers, and elsewhere as the symbol of the sport's future. He and his wife even appeared on the side of a box of Closeup toothpaste.

As Gordon was driving toward his championship, NASCAR was also developing two other projects—the Craftsman Truck Series and a chain of NASCAR Cafés.

In 1995, NASCAR launched the Truck Series to great fanfare and spectator approval. Racing on smaller venues around the country, the Truck Series was a way to bring big-league racing to areas not reached by the big boys of the

In 1998 Jeff Gordon appeared in Times Square, New York City, before receiving his third Winston Cup Championship award on ESPN. That year, during NASCAR's 50th anniversary season, he tied Richard Petty's record for most wins in a single season.

Winston Cup Series. The Truck Series took off, launching the careers of such drivers as Mike Skinner, Ron Hornaday, and Kenny Irwin Jr.

With the Cafés, the first of which opened in 1978, NASCAR put itself in competition with theme restaurants such as Planet Hollywood and the Hard Rock Café. Indeed, NASCAR was going from the track to the boardrooms and becoming a major presence in various forms of sports and entertainment.

The attention drawn to racing by booming television ratings and by stars like Gordon helped kick off a track-building explosion that continues today. In 1997 the Texas Motor Speedway opened in Ft. Worth. The addition of Texas, however, did not come without some pain. Because of NASCAR's tight schedule, just building a track no longer means a guaranteed date on the Winston Cup roster.

Texas owner Smith and New Hampshire owner Bob Bahre each bought half of another track—the North Wilkesboro Speedway, a tiny, .625-mile oval that had been part of the NASCAR family since 1949. But at the time NASCAR was growing incredibly fast, and the track's limited seating capacity and its closeness to larger facilities in Charlotte made it less desirable, so it became something of an outcast from the series. In 1996 North Wilkesboro had been home to two annual Winston Cup races. Now Smith and Bahre, who had hoped to add another race at New Hampshire, were out of luck. Without the Winston Cup race the men were essentially forced to close the facility.

Gordon, meanwhile, was proving his 1995 title was not a fluke. In 1996 he finished second to teammate Terry Labonte for the championship title. Following Labonte's title win at Atlanta in 1996, Gordon and several other top NASCAR drivers headed off to Japan for the first of three exhibition races there.

A year later, Gordon topped his runner-up status to Labonte by winning the 1997 title. He kicked off the year with a win in the prestigious 39th running of the Daytona 500, becoming, at 25, the youngest person ever to win the race. Since its inception in 1959, the Daytona 500 has become the crown jewel of the NASCAR series and gives the winner a lifetime of recognition for the feat.

Besides Texas, the 1997 outing also marked the opening of the California Speedway, in Fontana, California, a racing showplace built by motorsports legend Roger Penske. Gordon became the inaugural winner at the facility. Then in 1998, in what's best described as a dream season, Gordon became the most dominant driver on the track. He won 13 races, tying Richard Petty's single-season win record in the modern era, and won his third title in four years.

Gordon earned the crown during NASCAR's 50th Anniversary Season, a year marked by an immense marketing campaign to show America that NASCAR had truly arrived. Indeed, with Gordon as its champion and its best example, NASCAR proved it had come a long way from a sport created by moonshiners in the South to a national phenomenon ready for the next 50 years and more.

CHRONOLOGY

1947   Bill France gathers fellow race promoters for a December meeting in Daytona Beach; the group votes to form a national sanctioning body to oversee stock car racing; they name the organization the National Association for Stock Car Automobile Racing (NASCAR) and select France president.

1948   NASCAR is incorporated.

1949   NASCAR sanctions its first-ever strictly stock race in Charlotte, North Carolina; race winner Glenn Dunnaway is disqualified when his car doesn't pass a post-race inspection; Jim Roper is awarded the win; Red Byron is crowned NASCAR's first champion.

1950   The first-ever Southern 500 is run at the Darlington Speedway, the first paved track built for stock car racing.

1955   NASCAR expands its schedule to 45 events at 32 tracks; boat motor manufacturer Carl Kiekhaefer becomes the first racing team sponsor.

1958   The last race is run on a combination beach-road course in Daytona Beach, Florida.

1959   The Daytona International Speedway, a 2.5 mile-long track built by Bill France, opens.

1960   Lee Petty, father, and Richard Petty, son, finished first and second at a NASCAR series race, the first time a father and son have finished No. 1 and No. 2.

1961   ABC's *Wide World of Sports* airs a portion of the Firecracker 400 from Daytona.

1969   Superspeedway opens at Talladega, Alabama; several drivers boycott the race due to danger of increased speed.

1970   NASCAR sanctions its last race on a dirt track.

1971   NASCAR reaches a deal with R. J. Reynolds Co. to sponsor the series, renaming it the Winston Cup Series.

1972   NASCAR reduces its schedule to 31 races per season; Bill France Jr. takes over leadership of NASCAR from his father.

1979   The first live telecast of a stock car race from start to finish is aired by CBS.

1984   Richard Petty, King of Stock Cars, wins his record 200th race.

1988   Bobby Allison leads his son Davey across the finish line in the Daytona 500, the second time a father and son have finished No. 1 and No. 2.

1992   Richard Petty retires; founder William Henry Getty France dies at age 82.

1994   NASCAR stages its first race at the Indianapolis Motor Speedway, the home of Indy car racing.

1995   Jeff Gordon, 24, wins the Winston Cup championship, becoming the youngest driver to do so in the modern era.

1996   First-ever NASCAR exhibition race held in Japan.

1997   Jeff Gordon wins the Daytona 500, becoming the youngest driver ever to win the race; the Texas Motor Speedway and the California Speedway become part of the Winston Cup Series; NASCAR celebrates its 50th anniversary.

1998   Jeff Gordon wins his third Winston Cup title in four years.

1999   Bill France Jr. turns over the day-to-day operations of NASCAR to Mike Helton; NASCAR and Donald Trump reach an agreement to build the Trump Superspeedway in the New York Metropolitan area.

FURTHER READING

Center, Bill and Bob Moore. *NASCAR 50 Greatest Drivers*. New York: HarperCollins, 1998.

Golenbock, Peter. *The Last Lap*. New York: Macmillan, 1998.

Golenbock, Peter and Greg Fielden. *The Stock Car Racing Encyclopedia*. Indianapolis, Indiana: Macmillan, 1997.

Huff, Richard. *Behind The Wall: A Season on the NASCAR Circuit*. Chicago: Bonus Books, 1996.

Huff, Richard. *The Insider's Guide to Stock Car Racing*. Chicago: Bonus Books, 1997.

The Official NASCAR Preview and Press Guide. UMI Publications, Inc.

Richard Petty's Official Guide to 50 Years of NASCAR. Petty Marketing Company L.L.C. 1998.

INDEX